The Arkansas Crappie

The Arkansas Crappie

"How to Successfully Catch Crappie"

Johnny E. Ware II

"God that made the world and all things therein, seeing that he is Lord of Heaven and Earth, dwelleth not on temples made with hands;"

Acts 17: 24 (KJV)

Copyright

Copyright © 2017 by Johnny E. Ware II. All rights reserved. This book or any portion thereof may not be reproduced or used in any manner whatsoever without the express written permission of The Butterfly Typeface Publishing House Co. except for the use of brief quotations in a book review.

Printed in the United States of America

First Printing, 2017

ISBN-13: 978-1-942022-59-6
ISBN10: 194202259X

The Butterfly Typeface Publishing
PO BOX 56193
Little Rock, Arkansas 72215

Dedication

I dedicate this book to the memory of my 5th grade reading and comprehension teacher, Doris Ruffin. Mrs. Ruffin had a vision of me that I didn't understand until now. You helped me to believe in myself through my Creator.

Thank you, Mrs. Ruffin!

Purpose is the understanding of an act or belief that has to be accomplished by all humans in order to solidify an endeavor given to us by our Creator. Therefore, understanding that we all truly have a purpose while here on Earth is paramount. It is up to each individual to seek out their unique purpose and to pray to our Creator for the proper guidance in achieving His ultimate endeavor.

Before you can accomplish all, you must first understand and accept who you are as a child of our Creator and know that He resides in you.

-Johnny E. Ware II

Table of Contents

Introduction 19

Summer Time Crappie Characteristics.............. 21

Moon Phase and Moon Rise Theory's 25

Moon Rise, Moon Set & Moon Illumination 30

    Barometric Pressure 30

    Barometric Pressure Fishing Chart 31

    Wind Speed & Wind Direction 32

Summer Crappie on Rivers................................ 35

Summer Crappie in Lakes with Live Bait 41

Summer and Night Time Crappie from the Shore 46

Things to Remember... 55

About the Author 57

Foreword

I was impressed with Mr. Ware from the moment our paths crossed. His vast knowledge of information, passion for his people and his craft is truly infectious.

Mr. Ware's heart is a big one and it's evident in what he does.

Watching him interact with others and speak on his dreams for his people is to watch him come alive.

There are great things still yet to come from this man and I'm privileged to have a front row seat.

-Iris M Williams

Acknowledgments

There are a select few to whom I must recognize. These individuals helped mold my inquisitive mind. It all began with a cousin whom I have always admired and looked up to; James D. Ware. James became the first in our family to research the Ware lineage and he personally identified our origin while here in the United States of America.

James' work and persistence truly inspired and motivated me to excel in my own research and collected data.

Others who influenced my historical efforts were John Henrik Clarke, Dr. Delbert Blair, Cornell West, Malcom X and in particular a Caucasian teacher who told me that my race (Black People) only existed due to a curse.

It is now my endeavor to reach the subconscious minds of children and adults and create an example of positive influence within a wicked atmosphere of lies and deceit.

My Creator and Butterfly Typeface Publishing is indeed making my dreams a reality.

Thank you for investing in my dream.

-Johnny E. Ware II

"Out of all the experiences covered in my book, one of my most gratifying achievements involving fishing would be teaching a child to fish and enjoy the nature in our society. It is satisfying to me to teach a child different strategies in life to achieve ultimate success in whatever endeavor they take on, including how to feed their family. These strategies can also be applied to the challenges and difficulties experienced in life."

-Johnny E. Ware II

Introduction

Thank you for your interest in my collected data, that coaches inexperienced anglers and provides some elementary "how too" on being more consistent in catching summer crappie.

My purpose for exposing this powerful information is because of the difficulty in finding and catching summer crappie from the shore. In the southern United States, it's called *bank fishing*. Some inexperienced anglers have no clue where to start or what to look for. This is simply a guide to increase your creel and to do it more consistently.

The majority of these examples are indeed my experiences, during the 1980's and 1990's, as I traveled across the United States while pursuing my career. My professional career took me away from my favorite lakes back home that I had become accustom too. Therefore, I had to find different strategies to catch crappie more consistently because the environment was quite different. The biggest surprise was even though the environment changed sometimes drastically, I quickly noticed that the majority of the crappies characteristics remained the same. So I started a productivity diary. I was able to document several key notes that ultimately made a difference in my creel at the end of the day.

After several years of observation and documenting my experiences, I've found that my technique is what allowed me to become more consistent in my daily creels. The most inexperienced angler should be able to catch more crappie by following this simplified material. It is your responsibility to ensure that all the information shared with you is within state's rules and regulations. All the following information will include the effects from moon phase, wind direction, wind speed, water temperature, barometric pressure and the type of cover.

Chapter 1

Summer Time Crappie Characteristics

When it comes to understanding crappies, most anglers will tell you that this species of fish is one of the most unpredictable fish in fresh water. You can try to catch them in many different ways, but your success will not be consistent until you understand its behavior and even then you'll mess up from time to time. Crappie fishing in America and other countries has become one of our best past times. Like any other fish, crappie have normal characteristics that change during different events such as cold fronts, moon phase, pressure, clouds, temperature, bait fish behavior etc.... During all condition crappie, will always be easily spooked by any abnormal sounds that vibrate through the water ultimately causing crappie to hold tight to cover and stop feeding or cause them to evacuate the area until normal conditions return.

Crappies prefer a cool and highly oxygenated atmosphere when possible; some rivers and lakes are too shallow to offer these ideal conditions during the summer. In deep lakes and rivers, the water is much cooler at deeper depths, and bait fish are normally more concentrated. On most occasions when crappies are not feeding they need cover (shelter). In a "crappies world" cover has different terms such as a brush piles or Christmas trees submerged in deep water or any shade from a stick or docks. In other words, shade from a single stick in the water across the back of a crappie is considered cover to a crappie. (No artificial trees.) In some states the Game and Fish Commissions are submerging crappie sanctuaries made form PVC tubing. Algae will accumulate on the PVC tubing and the algae attract minnows and the minnows attract the crappie. It's called a crappie sanctuary because a crappie has ideal conditions; the water is

The Arkansas Crappie

cooler, there's plenty of cover and an unlimited amount of food.

In rivers and lakes crappies naturally preferred bait would be as follows: shad, skip jacks, minnows and sometimes insects, crickets, grasshoppers etc.

One important characteristic to remember about this species is crappie will not descend to feed. They will only feed below the prey they've seen. It is known as an ambushing prey. During the summer months crappie, will follow bait fish to the shallows also during the night and overcast, cloudy, days. During the heat of the day crappies are deep and even when they are not feeding they're somewhere close to the bait fish. In the river, when the flood gates are closed which means water is not flowing at all, crappie normally seek shelter under large boulders, under water rocked cliffs and concrete walls.

They frequently feed at night during the summer months in deep and shallow waters depending on bait fish temperature, pressure, and atmosphere and of course the moon phase. You have to be careful at nights during the summer depending on where you are fishing. In the south some states have to worry about snakes and alligators and also bears and moose in other parts of the country. At night, in deep water, lights can be submerged under water to attract bait fish then the crappie come in for the bait fish.

Chapter 2

Moon Phase and Moon Rise Theory's

Some of you will look at this section and ask, "What does the moon have to do with fishing?" Believe me, if you pay attention to the information that follows you can observe it for yourself through your own experiences. We all know that the moon's satirical force is responsible for the low and high tides of the ocean. Every being on earth is somehow affected by the moon one way or another and fish are no different.

When I was a young man I often heard my grandfather say, "The crappies are not biting today because their mouths are sore," I never understood what he and others meant by using that phrase. He would also say, "Baby boy, look at the cows lying down in the pasture." This meant the fish would not really be active that day. It didn't always mean we would not catch any fish. Grandpa said it just meant the fish would be lazy like the cows.

As a small child, I really didn't understand the meaning of many of the so called "old sayings." My grandfather was a very funny man so you didn't always know when he was kidding around. He used a form of amazing dialog to deliver a sincere message. The last phrase I remember my grandfather using was, "If the wind blows out of the east the fish will bite the least," and guess what - fish just won't bite when the wind is out of the east.

I can't tell you why, but all I can give you is the facts. Check it out! Oh yeah, guess what it happens when the cows lay down too. I have caught crappie when the wind was blowing from the southeast, west, south and north never consistently when the east wind was blowing. Now I have to evaluate wind and moon.

The moon seems to affect the fish on different phases of the moon. My rule of thumb is this: Every time the moon is going to be on the same side of the earth where I am fishing, I wait until the moon pattern changes before I take my trip or when the moon's illumination is less than 3% of a new moon.

- When the moon is illuminated 25% and it rises at 6:00am I will consider fishing from 6:00am until 10:00am because I can sometimes catch crappie until the moon reaches the ten o'clock position in the sky.

- When the moon is illuminated 50% or more and the moon rises at 6:00am normally I will wait to that particular phase is over. I just can't seem to tear them up when the moon is more than 25% illuminated and on the same side of the earth where I'm fishing.

- When the moon is fully illuminated (full moon) and it rises right before dark I can fish from that morning at daybreak all the way to dark with good success.

- When a full moon rises at 6:00am I will not fish the whole day until an hour before dark.

- The observation of the moon is not as important if there is an overcast twelve hours before you go up until the time you start fishing for some reason the moon doesn't affect them as much.

- I catch more fish during the new moon than any other time of any month. A new moon is when the moon is only illuminated 5% or less.

- When a full moon rises at 7:00pm and sets at 7:00am the next morning I will not even attempt to fish a minimum of six hours after the full moon has set. For some reason when the full moon illuminates through the night it seems that the fish feeds and won't feed again until a few hours after it sets.

You can read about my experiences as many times as you would like but until you start observing and documenting the conditions during each of your outings your creel will be inconsistent. Document the moon phase and moon rise, barometric pressure, wind speed, wind direction, clouds, sunlight and temperature.

All of this information you should know before you go on your fishing excursion if you're looking for consistency.

Chapter 3

Moon Rise, Moon Set & Moon Illumination

These three events can affect the crappie's behavior drastically such as causing them to become active and start a feeding frenzy or cause the crappie to show a lack of interest in your bait or lure. Sometimes they'll seek cover (shelter) and hold tight too it, until this period is over. The illumination from the moon also creates natural light for feeding at night and affects the crappies feeding patterns throughout the day.

Barometric Pressure

Somehow the Barometric pressure affects the crappie's behavior and their ability to swallow prey, and I truly believe that this is exactly what my grandfather was speaking of when he mentioned "the cows laying down in the pasture", and the "crappie's mouths were sore". Both statements indicating that the fish were not biting. I've often heard other anglers mention, when the Barometric pressure is high around 31 points, it causes the crappies lungs or stomach to expand, therefore enabling the fish to swallow or causing them to lose interest in feeding from a bloating sensation and assuming their bellies are full. When the barometric pressure is considered low, around 29 points, it seems like the fish will jump on the shore and really become quite active and will feed in frenzy like mode. Unfortunately, there's usually some rough weather that comes with it such as warm weather fronts and cool weather fronts.

Barometric Pressure Fishing Chart

29-29.9	30-30.9	31-31.9
Excellent	Average	Poor

Wind Speed & Wind Direction

Wind speed and wind direction can also play a big part in your success during the hunt for crappie or it can also deter your efforts. The results can only be determined through trial and error; sometimes it works and sometimes it doesn't, but you'll appreciate the experience.

For example, one day the moon phase was perfect in fact, it was a new moon. My son and I went fishing on the river in a cove where there was no flowing water at all. Right off the dam, where the water was flowing very hard (meaning the gates were letting a lot of water out). Crappie can handle the current but prefer feeding in calmer waters and calmer water is the ideal condition.

So, the cove was a refuge from the strong currents off the dam for bait fish and other species of fish also our famous crappie. Now back to the wind, the wind had been blowing approximately 35 mph all day, and the wind was blowing southwest, off the river and right into the cove. This meant that the wind blew hard into the end of the southwest corner of the cove, right into the shore with water up to 35 ft. deep. Getting to the cove involved a lengthy walk over the rocks.

There were different signs to consider before taking such a long walk:

- Was the water still rising?
- Could we see bait fish moving?
- Was the wind consistent?
- Could we make it happen?

Seeing the good signs, my son and myself proudly headed for the southwest corner of the cove, once we arrived we quickly realized the shad and skipjack (bait fish) were so thick that the whole end of the cove looked as if the wind had blown every bait fish in the river to the southwest corner of the cove.

Remember if you ever see bait fish in this manner, I guarantee you the predator known as 'the fish' are indeed somewhere near.

Need I say more?

The wind was blowing in our faces. My son used a 1/16oz jigs and a leaded float and fished about 4 feet deep. I freelanced with 2-1/16oz jigs and tied them about 12 inches apart.

We both had our limit of twenty slab crappies, within an hour.

Any shore that has a high wind blowing directly on the same, will hold bait fish and believe me the fish are near.

Remember when the wind is out of the east the fish will bite the least.

Chapter 4

Summer Crappie on Rivers

While hunting crappie during the summer you have to know that crappie are not as active during the hot days especially in shallow rivers because of the lower oxygen supply. My first move is to evaluate the moon phase calculator and if the moon conditions are ideal I make a trip to the deeper rivers because it's likely the fish will be more active in deeper depths. During the summer months, I choose my locations on shore by looking for deep water excess such as public fishing docks over deep water in cove and off of jetties on the river.

In some states the Corp of Engineers or Game and Fish Commission will submerge a structure in cover and bays on the river such as real Christmas trees, PVC piping and timber; even though this structure is considered cover for crappie and other species of fish.

These different types of structure will build up algae and algae will attract bait fish and in return bait fish will keep the crappie near. With both cover and food, crappie will remain in the area for long periods of time. Calm water is the key. Now that you know exactly what to look for in deeper rivers now let's focus on putting slab crappie in the fish basket.

There are different tactics you can try while pursuing crappie which can sometimes be finicky feeders. You can use live bait such as minnows, shad, waxworms, fresh water grass shrimp or artificial lures called crappie jigs and crank baits and spinner baits. We will discuss both methods of live bait and artificial bait in detail.

Be as follows, tackle is so important. Sometimes it is very confusing when trying to predict what color jig crappie will want or how deep they are and etc... and be prepared to change your tactic to stay with crappie.

When I'm fishing on the river and the water is flowing I use a jig with a lead head and a No. 2 hook. I use an 8ft graphite rod, a Mitchell Avocet II S-2000 reel and Stren 4lb test line depending how strong the current is I normally will use leaded jig heads sizes from 1/16 ounce, 1/8 ounce, 1/4 ounce. The color of the tube jig really depends on the clarity of the water. This technique is called "free lancing" a detail list of items used:

1 – 8ft Rod Graphite Micro Light Sensitive

1 – Mitchell Avocet II S-2000 Reel

1 – 200yd Stren 4lb Test Line

30 – Jig Heads 10 – 1/16oz: 10 – 1/8oz; 10 – 1/4oz

10 to 30 – Different color tubes skirts for jig heads

All these items can be found at your local stores. I would probably use 2 – 1/16oz crappie jigs tying them approximately 12 inches apart and finding my way to the best eddy that I can find and verify that the water isn't flowing in any direction other than a perceived look of boiling water.

The eddy normally always will hold bait fish and the crappie will come in to ambush them. As I check my two lures to make sure they are presentable. I then throw my lures into the perfect illusion of boiling water. As the two lures hit the water I begin my count. (If the sun is out and hot the crappie are pretty deep and if its winter or fall and the clouds are out crappie could be much shallower.) I count by starting with one thousand one, one thousand two and so on. One thousand one is equivalent to one foot of dissention meaning the lure is dropping a foot in depth on every one thousand count.

On the first throw, sometimes I will count until the jigs hit the bottom and get hung in rocks or sometimes you can feel the bottom through your line without it getting hung. When you count until you hit the bottom then you will know what count to stop your descent and start reeling in a slow fashion without allowing it to descend deeper.

When the fish attacks your lure you will feel a "thump" or "bump" through your line at the tip of your rod. I need to also mention once you've thrown your lures and they have descended to the depth that you want make sure you're holding your rod at a 45^0 angle as the lures descend. Sometimes the crappie will attack your lures as it descends so it's important to decrease the slack in your line so you can feel the fish bite your lures.

Sometimes when crappie are schooling and feeding; I can catch two crappie, at one time, using these two lures set up. The important thing to remember is the count that the fish hit your bait because that will be the depth that you will probably catch the remainder of your crappie.

Example: If you're counting as your jig descends and you are on count one thousand twenty-two when a fish strikes this means your bait was attacked at approximately 22-

25 feet deep so you should continue expecting the hit around the same count.

I will use this same technique throwing spinner baits such as the road runners, brettle spins or rooster tails. Crank baits at a slow retrieve will usually work. Bays and coves where there are no currents are great holding areas for crappie as well.

Chapter 5

Summer Crappie in Lakes with Live Bait

Live bait is most definitely hard to beat when it comes to consistent creels in lakes. Sometimes when crappies are not active; an artificial lure just won't work. During those inactive periods, I go to the best live bait ever known to man for catching these finicky eaters (crappie). This bait is known as the famous minnow. I have found that inactive, none feeding crappie just cannot stand a live frisky minnow that sets right in front of their face without being able to escape sooner or later they have to attack the minnow.

There's a very simple technique that I use to increase my creel during their inactive periods. First let discuss an example of how I form a strategy based on an ideal situation.

Example: Let's say I found a lake that has a public fishing pier that set over 30 feet of water. Below the pier the Game and Fish Commission has submerged brush and natural Christmas trees which is a very productive crappie sanctuary, perfect shelter or cover for crappie. The brush pile on the bottom of the lake stacks up about 10 feet off the bottom that would give you 18 to 20 feet of depth to fish without getting hung in the brush. Normally the fish are suspended right above the brush. Remember if bait is 10 feet above the pile the crappie will be right under the bait fish.

As I specified in an earlier chapter crappie are a very spooky species. Any abnormal noise or splash will move them out of the area or shut them down. If you accidently get hung in the brush, just leave it there and use another rod or pole and if you just have one pole just cut the line.

This is an itemized list for the necessary supplies I use when I am fishing with live bait.

The Arkansas Crappie

1 – 12ft Uncle Bucks Crappie Pole

1 – Mitchell Ultra-Light Reel

100yds – 4lb Stren test line

3 pack – Sup Floats

1 pack (24 count) – Slip Knots and Beads

1 package – 1/16oz Split shot Lead Sinkers

1 package – Gold No.2 Crappie Hooks by Eagle claw

Bait of Choice:

- 1/4lb of Rosy Pink Minnows
- 1/4lb Medium Silver Shiners Minnows
- 100 count Wax Worms

This tackle, not including real live bait, can be found at your local Walmart or bait shop.

The following is a simple diagram of my slip float set up. Some people say this tactic is confusing but it's not. It is quite productive and has the ability to go as deep as you would like without having to change your rig simply by sliding the knot up and down for the desired depth.

The slip float rig is a powerful strategy for deep water crappie. Just sliding the slip up or down will increase or decrease your depth. This strategy is also great when crappies are inactive if the minnow is lively; sooner or later the crappie will eventually attack your minnow.

One of the most effective producers would be hooking the minnow at the back of the dorsal fin. It allows the minnow to move freely and tease the crappie to attack.

SLIP FLOAT ILLUSTRATION

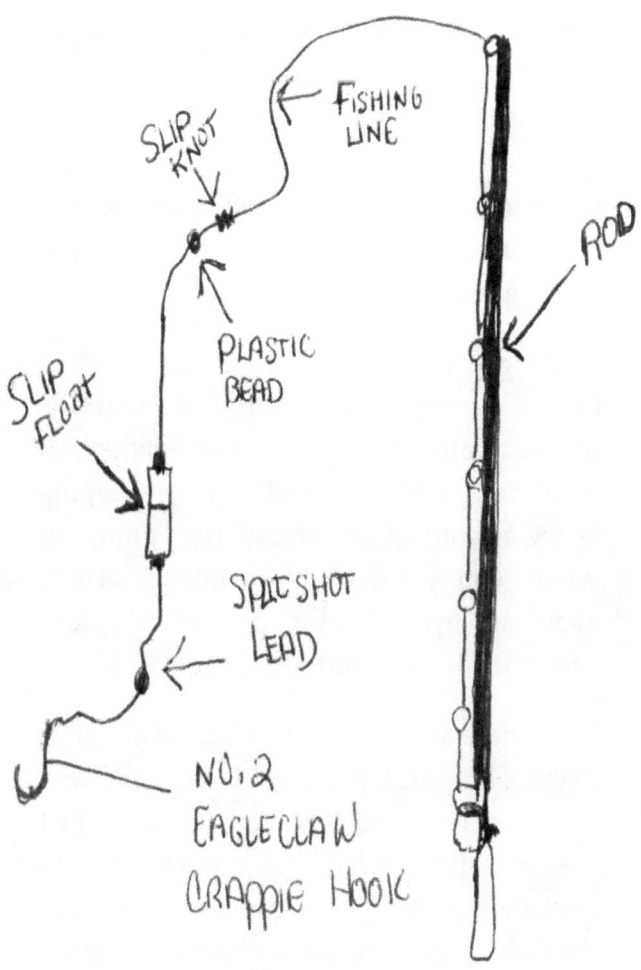

Chapter 6

Summer and Night Time Crappie from the Shore

Crappie fishing at night can really be fun and bring excellent creels during the summer months.

There are quite a few things to consider before making a trip. Safety of course is number one. Mosquitos and snakes to mention another and also keeping everyone out of the water. Depending on where you are fishing you might have to keep an eye out for a few alligators especially in the southern United States.

The whole secret for a productive summer night of crappie fishing would be "light" and a concentration of plankton, which is just the opposite of what they are accustomed to at night unless there are houses around the lake which doesn't create the same effect; the darker the surrounding areas around the lake the better. Your light will be more effective and produce good creels.

As I mentioned earlier, light is the magic for a productive night of catching crappie but there are other actions that must occur before you achieve your success.

The submersible light should be placed no more than 1 ft. under water, if you take it any deeper than that, you stand a good chance to spook this finicky fish. The submersible lights can come in different colors and some colors are more effective than others, depending of the clarity or the water itself. The submersible lights come in colors, such as green, red, and clear, but the most productive color for me in all conditions would be the green light, but do your own assessment of your favorite fishing hole to determine what's best for you.

The lantern is the other alternative while hunting crappie at night, My first experience night fishing was indeed with the lantern, (the original Coleman Lantern). The lantern was sometimes more productive than the submersible lights, because bugs and mosquitoes would hit the hot lantern and hit the water to attract a more natural setting for the haunted species known as crappie. The ideal settings for the lantern would be to stabilized it approximately 1 to 3 ft. above the water for best results, whether you hang it on a tree limb or hang it from a fishing doc. The most important thing you can do is to evaluate and document everything you do, and all the conditions that involved the success or failures.

For this example, let's use the same fishing pier discussed in Chapter 4 also use the same equipment in Chapter 4 as well. The slip float rig and vertical jig fishing technique can be used on this set up at night.

Additional Supplies Needed:

1 – Green, White or Blue Submergible light

1 – Head Light for your head with a Red Lens

1 – Roll of Kite String

1 – Gallon Clear Jar with a lid (pickle jar)

1lb – Rosy Pink Minnows and Tube Jigs

1 – Submergible Minnow Bucket

2 – 8ft Wood 2x4 Studs

1 – 30lbs Sand Bag

1 – Roll duct Tape

1 – Trolling Battery

1 – Foam Pad for Battery

1 – Five Gallon Bucket

Before I even plan my trip, I find out where the moon will be by going to the following website:
www.timeanddate.com/.../moonrise.html

This site again will give you the time the moon will rise and fall and also give you the percent of illumination, meaning that percentage of the moon that can be seen with the naked eye. I just don't do very well in producing good creels when the moon is present.

I always try to be at the lake a couple of hours before dark because it gives me plenty time to set up my complete thought out plan and I sometimes catch fish before dark. I will take both 2x4 studs that are 8ft each and tie the kite strings around one end of both studs and then tape the tied end with duct tape to secure the tied knot.

One stud's kite string should have 10ft of string hanging from the stud and the other stud should have at least 5ft of kite string hanging from it.

Now you should have two 2x4x8 studs, one with a string hanging 10ft and the other one with kite string hanging 5ft.

Next take the 1-gallon jar and fill it up half full of water from the lake you're about to fish and put 2 dozen rosy pink minnows inside the jar.

Take the lid to the jar and drill a 1/4-inch hole in the center of the lid then take the kite string that has the 10ft piece of kite string and start pushing the kite string through the center hole of the lid from the outside in.

Push approximately 6 inches of kite string through the 1/4-inch opening. Take the 6 inches of string and make continuous knots at the end of the string so the string will not come back through the hole.

Now take the lid and poke a few small holes and screw it back on the jar with the minnows inside.

Once you've screwed the lid back on tight put pressure on the string by trying to pick the full jar up by using string. Caution! If the knot isn't at least 4 or 5 times larger than the hole in the lid, you will lose everything!

Now take the 2x4 stud that has the jar tied to it and lay it down on the platform extending it over the water approximately 2 or 3 feet. Then slowly submerge the jar into the water. If you see a concentration of air pockets coming up usually it means the jar is filling up with water as it descends.

The Arkansas Crappie

Now cover the other end of the 2x4 stud with the sand bags I previously discussed to secure the stud. Take the other 2x4 stud with the 5ft kite string tied to it and lay it about a foot beside the other stud before you extend it over the water.

Tie the submergible light up to the string so that the light will be no deeper than 1ft under water. Do not turn the light on until 30 minutes after dark.

Bring your battery close by for quick access. Now you should have the 2 – 2x4 studs side by side no more than 1ft apart.

The jar of minnows should be 7 to 10ft under the light. If there's crappie already there in the brush pile below, believe me the minnows in the jar are teasing the heck out of the existing crappie.

Depending on the depth of the jar sometimes you can hear crappie pecking at the jar. The jar of minnows seems to create an artificial feeding frenzy.

Next go ahead and prepare two poles before dark one with the slid float rig and the other one with a 1/16oz crappie jig.

Now take your 5-gallon bucket and fill it half full of lake water so you can collect your fish without spooking the crappie in a fish basket.

Now it's 15 minutes before dark and you must be able to see your surroundings so it would be a good ideal to have your head lamp on using the red bulb. The red bulb will not spook fish.

Now you can plug your light into your battery and power the light to the on position. Notice there's an area around the light that is more illuminated which is about 5ft in diameter.

Start fishing in the area where the light starts to dim. I would start at a depth about 1ft above the jar of minnows first.

Now have some fun and don't exceed your creel limit. (Make sure this technique is permissible with the laws of the state where you are fishing.)

Things to Remember

- ☑ If the moon is up on your side of the earth (you can see the moon that night), don't go fishing that night!
- ☑ If the wind is blowing out of the east, don't go fishing that night!
- ☑ If the Barometric pressure is 31.0 points or higher, don't go fishing that night!
- ☑ If the water is extremely stained from flooded conditions, don't go fishing that night!

However, if you want to go fishing purely for the enjoyment, evaluate your trip and verify the experiences I've documented for you.

About the Author

During his youth, author Johnny Ware was a child who had more questions and genuine concerns than most children his age. He found himself attracted to the more mature individual's mindset and divine intellect which created a unique hunger for knowledge and understanding.

Considered unorthodox regarding his questions concerning religion and the origin of his people, many adults raised their brows towards him because they didn't understand.

In school, he was taught a curriculum in history that told of other religions and the history of other races, but for this country he only learned of slavery and the United States history. This left him quite ashamed.

Coming from the southern part of the United States, Mr. Ware appreciated the different environments that he witnessed through different settings and perceptions of his fellow Americans.

Now that he is an author, his mission is to communicate to the subconscious minds of others (especially children) through moral examples based on his belief of wrong and right rather than black or white.

After traveling throughout the United States for several years pursuing the American Dream, Mr. Ware absorbed a great deal of history and experiences that he plans to share with others.

Mr. Ware also writes in order to create an understanding for adults to realize that we all have a purpose here on Earth and it is therefore up to each individual to find their purpose and then pursue it to the best of their ability.

"I hope and pray that you find my writings a positive force in our society and in your lives."

The Butterfly Typeface Publishing House Co.

The Butterfly Typeface Publishing House Company is a full service professional publishing company. Our goal is to 'spread a message' of inspiration, imagination and intrigue in all that we do.

Whether you hire us to edit, ghostwrite, publish (books & magazines) or web design, you can be guaranteed exemplary customer service, fairness and quality.

Our vision, under God's leadership, is to serve and assist in the healing of the heart, mind and soul of *all* people we encounter with integrity, intentional influence and positive purpose.

"We make good GREAT!"

The Butterfly Typeface Publishing House Co
Little Rock Arkansas

www.butterflytypeface.com

www.ingramcontent.com/pod-product-compliance
Lightning Source LLC
Chambersburg PA
CBHW061253040426
42444CB00010B/2374